Some Girls

SOME GIRLS

✳

Janet McNally

The White Pine Press Poetry Prize, Volume 20

WHITE PINE PRESS / BUFFALO, NEW YORK

WHITE PINE PRESS   P.O. BOX 236   BUFFALO, NEW YORK 14201
www.whitepine.org

Publication of this book was made possible, in part, with public funds from the New York State Council on the Arts, a State Agency.

ACKNOWLEDGMENTS: Many thanks to editors of the following publications in which these poems appeared, sometimes in other versions: *Alaska Quarterly Review*: "Lilith, Happily." *Bayou Magazine*: "Eve Remembers What She Forgot." *The Buffalo News*: "Eurydice and Orpheus Stay Up Late." *Confrontation*: "Ariadne Knits." *Contrary*: "Demeter Takes A Walk," "Fins," "Multiverse," "Side Effects." *Crazyhorse*: "Maggie Says There's No Such Thing as Winter." *Ecotone*: "Eve and the Extinct Things." *Fifth Wednesday Journal*: "Archaeology: A Question." *Fourteen Hills*: "This Is Just an Experiment." *Frank Martin Review*: "Rapunzel on the Observation Deck of the Empire State Building" and "Aphrodite in Drag, Outside Grace Church, Manhattan." *Hayden's Ferry Review*: "Maggie Leaves the Underworld." *Mid-American Review*: "O" and "Saltwater." *The Mom Egg*: "Leda in My Kitchen." *Naugatuck River Review*: "Maggie and I at Summer Camp." *New Madrid*: "The Wicked One Goes to the Makeup Counter." *New Ohio Review*: "Circe and the Baby" and "Chimera." *Nimrod*: "The Maenads Go to a Meeting." *Passages North*: "Fairy Tales" and "Hecuba and Gravity." *Poetry Daily*: "This Is Just An Experiment." *Redivider*: "Eurydice and Orpheus Stay Up Late." *RHINO Poetry*: "Persephone Has a Secret" (as "Persephone is Pregnant") and "Mothers, We Are Gone." *Silk Road Review*: "Gretel Has a Garden Now." *So to Speak*: "Trompe L'oeil" and "Un-being." *Southampton Review*: "Scheherazade and Salome Share a Smoke, Backstage at the Gentlemen's Club" (as "Salome at Pharaoh's Gentlemen's Club"). *Southern Humanities Review*: "Thessalonike Leaves the Water." *Southern Poetry Review*: "Maggie as Sleeping Beauty" (as "Maggie"). *A Woman's Thing*: "My Next Heart." *Yemassee*: "Penelope and Oz."

Anthologies:
My Cruel Invention: A Contemporary Poetry Anthology (Meerkat Press): "This Is Just an Experiment."

Moonshine: An Anthology (Two of Cups Press): "Eurydice and Orpheus Stay Up Late."

Thanks to Matthew Dickman, who chose "Maggie Leaves the Underworld" for *Best New Poets 2012*.

Cover photograph copyright ©2014 by Brett Essler. Used by permission.

ISBN 978-1-935210-70-2

Library of Congress Control Number: 2014960007

I'm grateful to Canisius College and my wonderful colleagues and students there. Thanks to Jaime Herbeck, Sherry Taylor, and Lindsey Row-Heyveld for reading the manuscript, and to Brett Essler and Jodi Bryon for being great friends who are game for anything (the cover photo is their beautiful work).

Many thanks to the New York Foundation for the Arts for fellowship support in 2008 and 2015.

Much gratitude to Anne Marie Comaratta, who cheers me on in whatever I do; to Mick Cochrane, who has been a wonderful and supportive friend for a long time; and to Eric Gansworth, who offers insight with humor and kindness. Michael Estes is a patient man and a fantastic last-minute poetry consultant, and Rebecca Hazelton inspires me with her own work and her ability to give perceptive notes on mine.

I'm very grateful to Ellen Bass for choosing my book, and for her generous guidance.

Thanks to all the teachers who have supported me, especially Eileen Maloney, Sister Connie Marlowe, Sonia Gernes, William O'Rourke, Valerie Sayers, Joan Tefft, and Steve Tomasula.

Many thanks to Dennis Maloney and Elaine LaMattina at White Pine Press.

Much love to my parents, who have always encouraged my love for words, and my brother Patrick, who is just as excited about this book as I am.

To Jesse, my heart, and our three girls: this book wouldn't exist without you.

To my girls:
Juno Elizabeth, Daphne Ramona, and Luella Maeve.

One

Two

Three

Some Girls

One

It Took Her So Long to Wake Up

Back then I wondered where my friend was
while she was sleeping, what stories
had been slipped like lozenges
under her tongue. Did she try on lives
like dresses, then cast them off
at the foot of the bed? Did she eat
the red berries though she knew
they were poison, pull the glossed apple
down from the branch?
Maybe she plucked the wrong flower
from the field, took it home and plunged it
into a jam jar filled with water.
By the time she woke, the roots
would have come clean, dirt gathered
at the silty bottom the only sign
it had ever been earthbound.

Maggie Leaves the Underworld

We saw her for weeks in our dreams, a slim ghost
crossing the street in suede boots. Her strides

were plastic, doll-kneed, and the sidewalk
waited for her, bleeding purple

in neon. Quiet. Dead girls can come
back, hearts bruised as plums

on the orchard floor. Some secret flint
sparks their beating and those girls stretch and rise.

By spring, Maggie had thrown all
her miracles like white doves in magic tricks.

Her last dreams were wildflowers, dipped
in the useless pollen that gathers

on windowsills instead of bees' legs. She came
back, she breathed in, her slate eyes opened.

It was some kind of show. We presented
her to strangers, but she never told

the truth while we were listening. We asked her
to open her mouth

wide enough for us to see
the seeds strung like garnets

on silken thread. Imagine, we said,
her throat as it opens. Imagine everything

she had to swallow before she convinced them
to let her go.

The Rules of This Place

We give every princess a horse to ride, or a deer
when the horses run out. We've had requests for leopards
but leopards are unreliable: they purr like small motors
and can't stay out of the trees. Here, you can make your deer
chandelier antlers, or sequin rabbits in the dark middle
of a road. If you want to be an animal we can do better
than hibernation. We can do better than cartoon bear.
At night deer lie down on the highway, though nobody
asks them, and bunnies raise their babies in burrows
by the curbs. I feed them graham crackers and count
their blinks electric, shocks in the dark.

                                        So rub your velvet
against this oak tree, deer. Settle your haunches on asphalt
and wait for the cars to pass. This is hospital, not forest,
but no one has noticed. Visiting hours are over and I'm still
here. I see you chose leopard anyway, and you're up there
in the branches. I don't know if you'll ever come down.
But gravity seems safe; it still fastens my shoes to the floor.
Blink and I'll count you; hook your claws into the bark
and climb back down.

Maggie as Sleeping Beauty

When she woke from her coma, her pupils
     had grown larger, as if they had bloomed

          while she slept. Her hair kinked
     in pillow waves for weeks and sleep creases mapped

trails across her face. How could we tell
     if she was the girl we knew before? We couldn't

          ask her to show us where it hurt, because
     her bones had knit themselves back together.

We had to trust that she would remember
     what we did, though we had extra

          days and weeks spooled like old film
     in canisters. She missed those days,

stretched under a hyacinth sheet.
     And when she woke she tested the ground

          with her toes as if she didn't believe in it,
     as if it were glass or smoke or some kind

of water and she was hanging above it,
     waiting to fall.

Lilith, Happily

The second time they started from scratch,
rolling the clay with their own hands.
God sighed, his knees sinking into loose soil
beneath his favorite tree, holding one rib,
curved and tender, for its magic.

As for Adam, he was slow to spin
the potter's wheel, afraid she'd turn out
like the last one: long-limbed, furious, full
of wild laughter. But he wanted her, so he
got dirty, plunged his fingers into the earth.

When they finished, they stood back,
happy, and watched the second one's
first steps. She was a doll.

       *

Later, Lilith would laugh when she heard
about her replacement, all lolling eyelids
and too-wide mouth. By then she was sending
postcards, stopping at mailboxes
in dusty Midwestern towns. She leaned out
the window of her blue pickup just to feel
the sun on her shoulders.

And when she heard the girl had eaten
the fruit, Lilith smiled. Turns out she wasn't
a puppet on a string, but hadn't she read
Snow White? Even if you forget
the glass casket and pig's heart
in a box, apples from strangers
are never a good idea.

For the first time, Lilith considered calling.
Standing in a phone booth, she held
the receiver in her hand.
But who would she ask for?

＊

Now she lives near the Pacific with a
stuntman from the movies, makes jewelry
from copper and jade. Adam moved, she heard;
left no forwarding address. So it's strange,
she thinks, that it's him she remembers
as she watches manufactured accidents,
each phony explosion as unsurprising
as the death of a minor star.

My Next Heart

I.
Next time, make my heart paper.
Origami, perhaps: translucent, sharp-cornered,

recyclable. When I'm done, I'll press it flat
and tuck it inside

a grocery bag. A man will come to the curb
and haul it away.

Look, miracle. No more flesh, no
secret language

of rhythm and thump. Just folds
and corners and a knife-edge

crease: a perfect little machine
that does nothing.

Girl-quiet, bright
liar, you'd never know

what kind of physics
is buzzing inside.

2.
Next time, make my heart
sailcloth, hemmed

with racing stripes. Stretch it
triangular and I'll sleep

the flat, soaring sleep of the albatross:
weeks at a time, sun blinking

on and off like a Christmas bulb. Blue dark,
white light, black ocean. I'll dream

updraft and downdraft and skim
over fog. I'll know the risks, and I won't care:

a sailcloth heart might glide away
before I'm done with it. All it takes

is one breath to get it started.
Things can go so far on their own.

The Maenads Go to a Meeting

When we say we tore him limb
from limb, we mean he wanted to fall
apart. Then, when it was over, we put
our ears to the wet earth and heard nothing.

It's not true that we tucked fragments
of bone or cartilage into our purses
like relics. We left him behind.

We're just like you. There are things
we remember and things we don't.
When we drink cranberry juice and seltzer
out of our wine glasses, we miss
the Beaujolais glow. We arrange doughnuts
on napkins and wipe powdered sugar
on our jeans. Our coffee waits
on the hotplate, growing more bitter,
more black, and the subway train below us
shivers chairs across the floor.

We could line up here and say our names,
one by one, but it's easier to speak like this.
We'll embroider our stories on pillows,
neat rows of x's adding up to what
we've lost. We'll learn how to spin something,
silk or sugar; we'll take up the ukulele
or the harp. Most nights, our dreams
are tessellated with memories of him,
and we can never find all the pieces.

Eurydice and Orpheus Stay Up Late

Their first night back, they go to the diner
on West 14th in the Village. Eurydice orders
a chocolate milkshake and fries, sprinkles salt
across the table like she's building an ocean from scratch.
You never know when you'll need to sail away,
Styx-style, on a sea made of soft-rock radio.
Underground, they played mostly the Stones.

She's seen Orpheus try to pout like Jagger,
but he's too nice for that, or too stupid.
His *moves* are more James Taylor: floppy hair,
acoustic guitar. She's seen him clutch that Gretsch
as if it could be taken from him—and this
is the guy who let go of her hand. She wants
to tell him what it was like down there,
how she forgot how to take breaths, to chew
and to swallow. But the fries are tiny salt licks
and it's not so hard to start again.

Outside, an eyelash sliver of moon
rests high in the west and she does the turning
this time, toward the steps down to the R train,
where that tunnel vanishes. Home?
She stands at the edge and expects to disappear,
to Ruby Tuesday her way right out of there.
It's a surprise when, this time, he grabs her hand
and pulls her back. The itch of her memories
recedes like a tide. The railing waits, wearing
a filigree of rust, but she holds on to him.

Penelope and Oz

Was it wrong to love that black-and-white
world? It seemed safe to her, first when she
was a girl and later, when she watched him

leave, her feet in the water and her hand raised
in a half-wave. You can wish against tornados
but they still pick you up, carry you

to a place where the Technicolor is so sweet
it hurts your teeth. You can stroll down the yellow brick
with a band of eccentrics, but at the end

you'll be alone, waiting with a tapestry
woven backward and a flock of dead geese.
She watched that movie and wondered why Dorothy

didn't hunker down till the cyclone winged away.
Better to keep to reliable gray; better to wait
for the day when only a house will hold you down.

Leda in My Kitchen

With her fingers flat on the table, her hands
feathered like a pair of wings, tips pointed,
a silvery shade of white I recognized
from somewhere else. Alabaster, or the concrete
spread of sidewalk soaked in moonlight. The idea
of a cloud in childhood, more insinuation
than weather. Book-ended, always,
by wakefulness and sleep.

She closed her eyes and said, *What bothers me most
is that I can't remember.* She held the curve
of her belly and I saw her fingers
were bone and skin again, pressed together
like a prayer. For a moment, we pretended
the egg in front of us had lost its terrible promise,
cradled no life in its calcium shell.

Rapunzel on the Observation Deck
of the Empire State Building

She sees night rise from the city
   though all the lights
   are on the ground:
      no stars, no moon

     in a graphite sky. The whole
   island a riot of neon and incandescence:

    Manhattan refusing to admit
   entire galaxies once spun
    in the arced sky above it.

(The half-life of memory
   is sometimes forget.)

   The city is cheap backdrop, starlings
     flying ballets
       through a stage-set
       sky, but she feels

  if she were to drop

something—a feather, a piece
of ribbon—
    it would hang in the air
    a moment
      before it fell.

Let down, let down, he said,
                    the first time
                    they met.

        She remembers it as *let go.*

Dangerous Electric

I once loved a boy who built batteries
for pacemakers, miniature machines
that could glint a heart to life.

      There were no secrets
      in his fingertips; to make sure,
      I held them to the light. Even so,

he had learned a way
to make a pulse. He might have
set it down like a wind-up toy:

      a small bear stomping
      across the table, escape
      on its mechanical mind.

Now, my own steps stutter
when I sneak into the hospital
and figure out how

      to bring you back. With me
      comes every girl I've ever been,
      holding hands to let

the current shiver through us
like spun sunlight: flaxen, fizzy,
a memory of miles, of measure,

      time tangled together, copper wires
      in my palm. Hello, gorgeous,
      give me your hand.

We've been waiting
for you. So rise, girl.
Wake up.

Eve Remembers What She Forgot

One bird with indigo wings
who always woke before the others

and searched the dew. I loved her
patient embroidery, moving insects around

in the too-green grass. Her voice, echoing
like a spoon scraping the bottom

of a porcelain bowl.

When I dream
of the garden, it's just a shoebox

diorama: flat cerulean sky, sweet
crayon colors of trees

and that blue, blue

river. Shadows belong to wind
or gravity: leaves

falling, waxy petals, branches

shifting softly in the breeze. We left
so quickly, and I swear

I gathered all that I could carry.

I turned to look back
until everything green was gone.

Now, that bird waits in saplings

draped in perpetual
spring. It's exhausting, all that

blossoming, day after day.
Her voice lost in botanical

rustling, her feathers sheening sapphire

in the light from an acquiescent sun.
Late morning, every morning,

she flits from tree to sky, wondering
why the world has been emptied

of every free-moving thing but her.

Maggie Says There's No Such Thing as Winter

If you believe in snow, you have to believe
in water as it's meant to be, loosed

from clouds arranged like asphodel. Because that's
what it's like to come back: a slow

surfacing, memory spiraling away. You can sleep
so long, whole seasons are forgotten

like hospital-room plaster, spidered
with cracks in Portugal shapes. You can love

sleep like water, love your heavy limbs
pushing river and ocean aside.

After Maggie woke, the doctors had her stringing
bracelets of semiprecious beads, and she

couldn't stop counting the kinds of blue.
Here, summer, in the high shade of a gingko,

she pulls up a handful of stones on silk
and we drink grapefruit seltzer, listening

to the tinny chime of bubbles
rising to the air. She can't remember

autumn, so we tell her someday this tree will drop
its fan-shaped leaves all at once,

golden in the October crush
of every plant's frantic strip show. Later

we'll see mountains through the scrim of empty
branches, and if we want we can look straight up

into the atmosphere, see the same plain old sky
revolving. When we ask Maggie what color it is

she always says iolite, picturing beads
like raindrops, shining azure on the table.

She forgets that sometimes things don't stay
where you leave them, that the sky fades

to white even before snow begins
to fall. It's hard, but we have to tell her

even sapphires don't glow blue
without some kind of help.

Two

Persephone Has a Secret

Everything's about to pop. The pollen
shakes like confetti from the long, red throats

of trumpet flowers. The air burns gold.
In this version, Hades is bayou Louisiana,

and the underworld drips
with rainwater and dew. She's the one

who's done it, loosed this place
from its ashen dusk the minute that child

started swirling beneath her rib cage, pulsing
like a flock of juncos winging in the trees.

Tonight, Luna moths gather on screens, their chartreuse
wingspread fragile as rice paper. They have

no mouths, no stomachs, and will live a week
and die. You've come to the right place,

she tells them. Here, you can go right on breathing
after you're dead. Not that she plans on staying.

For now, she's naming the flowers
as they sprout: pink stars of seashore

mallow, white jasmine trailing leaves
in brackish water. Hibiscus so red it slows

the amnesia flutter in her blood, lets her remember
the single bloom that stole her soul in the first place:

narcissus, pinwheel blossom, sepals
and petals both crushed in her astonished grasp.

From the turntable, Nina Simone sings
"Lilac Wine." Another flower she'll show

her baby, another word she'll spell
when they step out of this place stone free.

O

It's a lot to ask the hips to separate, to make room,

secret bones unhinging. The pelvis a door

to get from there to here. Did you run your fingertips

across walls as you passed through, searching

for a window, a light switch? Maybe you tucked

your chin and closed your eyes, tried to dream.

When your lips touched the air you opened them,

made an O like you'd practiced. With your eyes

on the ceiling, the lights, a bloom of oxygen

filled your lungs. I remember the ways

my bones fit together when I was eleven,

practicing pliés on the barre in our basement.

My open knees made a halo of my shadow

on the floor, and every time I reached

the concrete, I pushed back up. This is only

an echo of everything.

Fairy Tales

I have a girl and immediately I think *wolves,*
apples, goddamned Hades rising up from a flowered
field. I want to hide the mirrors, the spindles;

smooth the sheets of every third bed. I can't un-read
these stories, pages sticky with honey
or milk, stand-ins for blood and the sweet

curve of bone. The darkness is full of people
breathing and the sky is too large, too empty.
In my dreams, she's Little Red, her cloak

like a comet's tail. Then she's the comet,
trailing ice and dust. This is what
I'll tell you: paper burns and books

can be closed, put back on the shelf.
When she moves fast enough to keep
from getting hurt, all they can do is follow.

Little Red Cap at Our Lady of Perpetual Help

When I finally bled, I wished I'd chosen
another color. I grew tired of red. My mother
told me to stay eggshell, alabaster,
mother-of-pearl. So I keep a bottle
of sunscreen in my third-floor locker,
and pour small cartons of milk
over my shoulders in the shower. It cools
the constellations of my freckles,
star-scorched spots I've had since birth.

Our school has marble stairs and I'm wearing
three-inch heels, but I don't see the trouble.
I'm not planning to run. In physics, we learn
about terminal velocity, but I know
there's no way for me to approach
that kind of speed. Especially now
that the boys have gone past the woods
to other buildings, each room
with a crucifix and gold-painted door.

I wait under the statue of Our Lady
and gather the stars around her skirt, careful
to hear their hiss on my skin. They form whole
novas like the gleam of animal eyes. Tidal, I pull
the moon back toward Earth. I call everything
home. The wolves here are not shaped like bodies.
There are no grandmothers here.

Maggie and I At Summer Camp

Forget the badminton nets strung like spider silk
through the trees, canoes bobbing lazily
in flat blue water. Plums and cherries on metal plates,

    sailcloth on tables, beetles on leaves.

You and I shadowed through the summer, flags crumpled
in our palms. We knew how to weave a bracelet
to get out of there, how to start a fire with our teeth. We knew

    the secret click the boys' bunk door made

when it closed after midnight, buried in cicada whirr
and exhaled dreams. We lay down in grass for those boys,
in clover, the honeyed white flowers

    a veil over the field and all the bees asleep.

The moon was a mirror, a borrower of light, but I'd forgive you
for thinking it was an ordinary girl. I can still see the dirt
under your nails and your feet in the river. Your name

    in the mouth of that boy, him saying your name.

Trompe L'oeil

Here is a quarter and here is no quarter. Choose a card
and I'll see if I can make it disappear. In the next-door
universe, I'm standing over Horseshoe Falls
but I've forgotten the barrel. Later, I'll use every mirror
in the house to make sure I'm still here.

Would the story be different if someone else
told it? You might listen better with a fist full of rabbit ears.
I'm dreaming, I'm damseled, I'm floating three inches
over the floor. It's amazing, but I'm still here.

When I see *sleight of hand* I think reindeer. When
they lock me in a box I hum. No, I drop
through the bottom and wait. There's a blue ceiling
over the stage to keep ghosts away, flecked with shy polish
of painted-on stars. They look real enough to burn
through the curtain at the end of the show. I've learned this
by so many times trying: you can saw a girl in half
but then you'll have two half-girls, and
what the hell good is that?

Un-being

Inside that Chinese lantern, you folded
    your limbs like a seedpod, zipping a line
        down your center. Fibonacci appraised you,

    nautilus, with the tiniest of tape measures.

The sway of my body was a sea holding you, houseboat,
    rocking the same path next to the shore.
        Now you wake squalling. Sweet palindrome,

    you saved all your vowels for the underbelly of your cry.

But where were you before that? Before you blipped
    into existence, before the blood swished in your ears
        like highway traffic at night.

    Before you slept, a pearl in my belly.

I know: at the edge of the galaxy, twisting
    in eddies of violet light. Star-born, nebula-nursed,
        you worked each element

    hydrogen helium oxygen carbon

in the blaze of your own heat. Nothing could hold you
    and nothing did. You swam, formless; you kaleidoscoped
        through black space sieved with light.

Circe and the Baby

She's certain it was once there.
        She had a sonogram
                like a square
of sky—dangerous weather
            gathered in the center of starless black.

But it wasn't weather at all, nothing
        so ephemeral. It was small
            and sturdy: little avocado,
      mouse heart, the last
ingredient for a complicated spell.

She still wonders what made it
            disappear. A magic
trick, a harmless charm. A silver dollar
      pressed inside your fist.

She claims enchantment
        and refuses to remember
            the day he left, when she stood
near the sea, the bitter taste
of blood like metal
        in her mouth.

The way she couldn't make
        either of them stay.

Demeter Takes a Walk

There was a time when she let things die.
They hadn't known how, before, and so
she taught them: bent the snapdragons

toward the earth with her own fingers,
shriveled their petals to brown. Parched leaves
rattled on the trees, a loose new sound,

another job for gravity. Her girl was gone,
but no one listened. They were too distracted.
Women wandered aimlessly, carrying

withered grapevines, baskets of rotten fruit.
The knockout roses held on for as long
as they could, but now they were only

stem and thorn, red globes of rosehip
spiked with vellum. Now, she knows
something small enough to fit in your palm

can let them keep you: juice-jeweled,
scarlet, fizzing with the shock of being
gone. Every footprint you left

rises in the field, and ghosts
are the only ones who don't have
to worry about spring.

Mothers, We Are Gone

The way out of the woods is an amber
flash of light. Why do we forget this
as soon as the leaves fan closed?
Let's stay where the sod offers crabgrass
and daisies, dandelions not yet gone
to seed. The forest yawns wide
and then narrows, oak roots snarl
through the soil. Watch for nets
of ivy, for juniper studded
with myrtle. We won't escape
this gilded aviary, this birdsong,
fern-frond, dark echoing brook.
The smallest of us will star handprints
in shore moss, five faint points
for no one to see. Back home,
our mothers will caress the black glass
of night, obsidian made of anger, cooled
in river stone shapes. They'll hum songs
that crumble long before they reach their ends.
All the wrong birds will hear their dreams.

Saltwater

Grainy and aquatic, you moved on the wide screen
of the ultrasound, your fingers like anemones

in an amniotic sea. You were the real mermaid,
your limbs rippling like kelp, your feet a fishtail

pressing against my ribs. You learned the stories
you would later need, practiced speaking

a language without words. You opened your mouth
and swallowed; you dreamed of somersaults

and sighed into the water. When I finally held you,
you blinked your eyes at the light

and the air. Your mouth opened slowly, tongue searching
for the water, for the last perfect grains of salt.

Mama, you said. *I had the strangest dream.*

This Is Just an Experiment

They let us girls start fires
in beakers, flinting matches ·
against our gray flannel skirts.

Bright sky opens beneath
the dropped ceiling, soft weather
swirls vertical in the space

between chairs. At the boys' school,
they used to kneel on marble
and tent their hands in prayer.

We burn our badness out
with small effigies of empty space.
We measure wingspans of birds

who crash into our windows;
we grow like lupines, leaf-deep
in weeds. We can share the hot

heat of our skin, our terrarium
dreams. We can bend a thin filament,
cajole a current's wary flux.

And someday, we'll build
the perfect girl: String her limbs
on silk ribbon, pencil eyebrows

with a No. 2. We'll ink diagrams
on tracing paper, hinge her ribs
with black elastic. She'll run

on nuclear fusion, solar power,
or a plain old three-prong outlet.
Keep your distance;

there's some rigging involved.
You'll lean in and she'll spark
without warning.

We can't be responsible
for what might happen
if you sit so close.

Side Effects

They say magic doesn't come free,
and you're beginning to believe it,

every day brushing tinsel
out of your hair. You wanted to wake

when they said you wouldn't, wanted to see
salt-white ceiling-sky every April morning.

Now that you're back you can smile
and let the smallest birds

sew you clothes, weave twine
and foil into your hair.

This world isn't the way you left it—
it's all cigarette ash and museum hush—

and you've come home with props
from other lives: eggshells and narcissus,

the occasional piece of fruit. But you can
leave behind the pomegranate juice, the scarlet

curve of Fuji apples. The stuff of other girls' ruin.
Forget whatever shattered heels

you ground down into the dirt,
but know your limbs will always be heavy

with sleep. You'll spell siesta, hum
slumber. Your mouth full of rose

petals, your eyes wide as stars.
Sometimes in the night you'll whisper,

Briar, briar, take me back.

Three

Filmstrip

They showed us the Ideal Girl
in a filmstrip, threading the tape

over a Catherine wheel. These
are the fireworks we'll remember, the sparks

that slow the singe behind our eyes. *Fight fire
with fire*, you said, *or else*

cocktails. In a bar on Diversey, a man
we didn't know came up and kissed

the side of my neck, then left.
Just walked straight out the door.

You saw and crossed the room
to me, martini

sloshing over the rim of your glass,
a small and cloudy sea. You touched

your fingers to my skin as if he'd left
something, but when I looked

in the mirror,
I couldn't find a mark.

And later, when a sunrise like a bruise
opened over the buildings,

we passed through the city
as credits rolled. You crossed the street

against the light and ran, laughing,
leaping up the curb as a taxi slid by.

I swear I saw you turn golden, Maggie,
but that could have been the film burning.

Archaeology: A Question

I.
What if she had slept
forever? The glass casket
prisming the light

of a thousand sunsets,
the little men watching her
melt to nothing

but long ivory bones.
They wanted a socket
to plug her into,

wanted a bell jar seal.
The prince showed up late
and turned away, ashen.

His hair had no time to turn
green. So the men buried her,
filling the space

around her ribcage with soil.
They scattered grass seeds
like wedding rice, and forgot.

2.
It's up to us to excavate her,
so we spread our tools
on the grass—tiny brushes, silver

shovels—and work until the sky
falls apart, pinking
its clouds in chalk colors.

A skeleton can be anything: serpent,
sea monster, spine-long
in the loam. But she's left

only calcium, phosphorous,
sodium in sprinkles. No stories.
Even the apple is gone, fluorescent

as a dream. If she were here, we'd
smooth her hair with the poison
comb, and it wouldn't hurt.

But instead we gather the bones
in the soil, luminous as shells.
We pick up the pieces.

Scheherazade and Salome Share a Smoke, Backstage at the Gentlemen's Club

So much of it is being quiet,
but Salome likes to talk. She'll tell me
her dance is a story, each veil
a chapter, gossamer and sheer.
I'll say *flimsy*, she'll say
diaphanous. Slowly.

Here in the half-light, I tell her
I've had enough of stories.
In the end, they can't save you
unless you learn to resist
the silvery lure of sleep.
Insomnia will soften
the corners of the room
like spider webs, and the men
will lean forward in folding chairs,
yawning.

Salome wishes she were barefoot,
but my eyes have adjusted to the half-dark
and the way the mirror-ball spangles
linger on my retinas. I'll see them
later in constellations when I
close my lids at the makeup table:
Andromeda, Cassiopeia, the Pleiades.
A bunch of girls in trouble
in the sky.

There are other ways to die.
The platters are all stainless
steel now. Our mothers

have long since given up
polishing silver.

Thessalonike Leaves the Water

What happens to a mermaid when she dries
out? Silver scales fade to skin, legs split

from tail and you start to cross them, carefully,
ankle over ankle. You can learn balance

without forgetting how to swim, but it's best to stay
out of the water. You can suck on coarse salt,

crunch the grains between your teeth like sand, but eventually
you'll have to quit with your hands in the spice cabinet,

your bare feet on the kitchen floor. Breathe deep:
there's so much air you'll never run out.

So why is it in every dream you're arcing
through the late morning fog, safe between

the rocks? The ocean wants you
because you're the one who can coax

the coral into bloom, the one who can save
this whole sea in the span of a single breath.

Ariadne knits

on Friday nights, with fuchsia wool
so bright you'd think she just sheared a flock
of alien sheep, bleating in zero gravity.
Their sky is purple with twin spinning moons,
and at dusk they blend right in.

There was a moment when a ball of string
was her future, held like a wedding bouquet.
She waited two days, her back pressed
against the hedges of the labyrinth,
leaves spilling over her shoulders. Inside,
the monster breathed its last breaths, and the man
who would leave her walked on tiptoe,
his eyes open in the terrible dark.

If she had used the thread
to make something, she would
at least have a cap or a sweater
whose cuffs would cover her wrists.

But she made nothing then,
or just after, when she watched his ship
kiss the horizon. Now she knits
with us, using yarn pink as sunrise.
Only scarves, which go in one direction:
always leading the way out.

Gretel Has a Garden Now

Starvation is a kind of music, a hushed
        worry, rust in the mouth. You lose your place
                in the middle
           of a story, and soon the maples are your only
secrets: their empty branches
           shelter, their rough bark
       solace. The black forest

           welcomes you in, showers you
       with the winged seeds
           of pinecones. Then you realize
it has nothing else left.

That was a long time ago. In this life,
       I have fences. I have dirt, mixed
           with crumbled peat and compost.
Blackberries and corn,

       Brandywine tomatoes
           like fat red hearts. I have bags of bone meal
                sinking heavy into dew-soaked grass.

       I think, sometimes, of the cows
                    who fell
when everyone starved. We turn their bones
to dust
       and feed our plants.
                The sun glitters in the soil.
       A small apology

for a world that whittles you from the inside out, leaving
       your bones, hooves, teeth
           in pastures where

you used to chew dandelions,

believing every day,
there would be another
        one to follow.

Hecuba and Gravity

When she was young, she saw Hokusai's prints of Mt. Fuji,
its peak a gentle slope in red ink and gray. Snow-pink
spring trees, diamond-sharp kites on fine black strings.
She wanted to unfasten the clouds, peel the whirling birds
away from their updraft spins. She couldn't quite love
two dimensions. So she folded squares of paper
into animals—here, a pointed shoulder, there,
a triangle of ear—and set them on a windowsill.
Sometimes the wind made them flutter to the floor.

Which is to say, she always knew what would happen,
if only in her sleep. In her dreams, the baby falls
like the cherry blossoms she's never seen.

The Wicked One Goes to the Makeup Counter

You can't argue beauty's not an accident, the particular heft and angle
of a chromosome's spin. A tarted spangle, bright lanyard twist, the slip
of cells weighting this boat uneven from stern to prow. We're all

skittery as marbles on a marble floor. Beauty stays, then goes;
it *fades*, we say, something about years and sun, the nights we slept
in makeup and left mascara like ashes on the pillowcase. We burned

through every one of our dreams. I wasn't always a stepmother, you know.
There were whole years when I was a girl. But now, these ladies
sell me moisturizer, stand close in their lab coats, pretending at science

in a fog of perfume. They wield a contour brush and my cheekbone pops.
The magic settles uneasy; it turns out fairy dust was always
fake. And the lipstick's made from beetles, shells crushed vermillion.

My color is Fleshpot, they say, it's Folie or Fixation. It's Wilderness;
it's Artificial Earth. They can't quite make themselves care.
We'll waste it, they know, whatever we've been given.

When Maggie Holds My Daughter

This room might be Delphi, late afternoon
light burning through the window, pooling gold

as syrup on the floor. And you might be
the Oracle, holding my girl like a laurel
branch, divining. You might know

how to read the flames. So,
Oracle, tell me

nothing will break her, nothing
will make her splinter like we did, into a hundred
other girls. Tell me her hummingbird

heart will keep flickering, blurred wings
behind her ribcage. Tell me I can keep her

safe. Tell me someday, she'll draw you
with a suitcase in your hands and a cloud
over your head, floating

down charcoal roads, across green
crayon canyons. Because I know
you're going to leave. And there goes

our plan to start dressing
like Stevie Nicks in our fifties, all top hats
and gypsy skirts. We were going to

sing "Rhiannon" from highway
car windows, ring like bells

through our own black nights.
But you are the one

who came back, and you
are better than nothing. You always said

you'd never be a mother, but now

you lift my baby, breathe
on her forehead like a blessing. You say,
Try not to screw this up.

Aphrodite in Drag, Outside Grace Church, Manhattan

Late March and the magnolias are blooming early,
a cellophane memory

you can pull from Louisiana to hold
over Broadway's wide avenue, layering it
beneath the hooked arches

of this church. The magnolia of your childhood
spread twenty feet from branch to branch,
holding handfuls of opalescent petals

aloft to the sun. *So showy,*
your mother said. *Has that tree no shame?*

Every spring she swept from the driveway
a mess of white, bruised magenta
in spots and clinging to the earth.

She let you wear your sister's
skirt if you stayed inside
the fence and your father

was at work. You stood beneath the tree
and pulled the blossoms down.

Now, outside this church, you find the trees
a prayer: Let the flowers coral the sky,
let their saucers hold rain

and pour it out on the grass.
Though in this city the grass
is mostly concrete,

and the sky is edged in lithium
silver, blushing in skyscrapered
squares. You'd like to say

love is as pliable as modeling clay, but really
it's more like the river rocks
your mother found on the shore

and, later, pulled from her pockets
to line the windowsills. She filled
her drawers, weighted the house-

plants with stones. Her habit
finds its way through blood: you're happy

every time you discover pockets
in the seams of your dress; you know sea glass

from gravel in full sun. And even now,
you walk through the city looking for something
to pick up, something to hold.

Chimera

Daughter, I read that you left part of yourself
behind, a slip of cells in my bloodstream like sugar.
Like silver glitter in snow globe water, moving lazily
in secret currents. Drop the sailboat into the river
and watch it glide.

Now that you're out, these cells stay gentle,
waiting like piles of shaken salt. I'm sure they have some
secret business in spaces I can't see. They hum a little song
with no melody and practice Morse code in heartbeat rhythm.
Hello hello, they say. I think it's some kind of goodbye.

Multiverse

For Betty

The years are a starry
river, too deep

and bright to cross.
Some stories I have

to make up: your first
girl and her blood

spinning to rubies,
beautiful and useless.

Bad fairy singing
songs into her

seashell ear, wolf-
fogged breath

on her window.
These stories come

untrue when we tell
them, transforming

as words unspool
from our tongues.

I dream you winding
the thread around your

fingers, pushing it
to the bottom of a

zippered pocket. I wake up
and check every coat.

Eve and the Extinct Things

Somehow she finds herself back in the garden, waking
at sunset in a patch of cry violets and Cuban holly.

The dew has already settled and her skin is damp.
It's only a memory of moisture, left from last time,

when everything was wet and everything was new.
Now: what? Old? You could say *ancient*, you could say

forgotten. In any case, a kind of dead. She always
liked the animals best, and they know it, coming close

now to circle her spot. A bird the size of a collie
walks an unsteady path through the grass and places its beak

in her hand. A dusk-colored leopard jumps from earth to branch
and she tips her face up to see it. There will be many days.

She will welcome the rest when they come, the tips
of her fingers brushing against their feathers or fur.

She'll lie down and tell them what it's like to begin
something, since all they will know is the end.

Fins

Sometimes I dream you're one of those Florida
mermaids in highway towns, slipping your legs
into a green iridescent tail. You kick past coral
reefs built from scaffolding, pearly conch shells
hiding the metal. You swim behind plate glass
and sneak hits of underwater air.

This is the breath you've been missing, Maggie,
this is the salt you wanted on your skin.
You know I imagined my daughter swimming
before she was born, and I saw the pictures,
her pretty limbs

tucked like petals over her body. Still, she'd have
sunk beneath her bath if I'd let her, lullabied
by her own memory of water. But I knew how
to keep her safe, if only in that one way. We say
we can't believe you left again, but the truth is,
you never really came back. So I dream you
behind glass, behind silk curtains

like the sails of some expensive boat. I dream you
with the sort of fins that let you touch
down on the tank's sandy bottom
as if you're landing on the moon. In the last act
you'll swim with minnows silver as spoons

and you'll push toward the surface, looking up
at the sky. Outside the tank: palm trees, plastic
flamingos, a half-translucent sun. And you,
head above the pool, hair dripping, telling me
you always knew how to breathe underwater.

Notes on the Poems

"Lilith, Happily": This version of Eve is after Anne Sexton's "Snow White."

"This Is Just an Experiment" is for Michele Pritchard.

"Chimera" refers to microchimerism, in which a mother retains in her body a small number of cells from her babies after they are born.

"Multiverse" is for my grandmother, Elizabeth Thompson Lewis.

Janet McNally is a poet and novelist who teaches creative writing at Canisius College. She has an Master of Fine Arts in fiction from the University of Notre Dame and has twice been a fiction fellow with the New York Foundation for the Arts. Her young adult novel, *Girls in the Moon*, is forthcoming from HarperCollins in early 2017. Her poems and stories have appeared in publications including *Boulevard, Gettysburg Review, Crazyhorse, Mid-American Review, Ecotone,* and *Best New Poets 2012*. She lives in Buffalo, New York, with her husband and three daughters.

Author photograph: Jesse Mank

THE WHITE PINE PRESS POETRY PRIZE

Vol. 20   Some Girls by Janet McNally. Selected by Ellen Bass.

Vol. 19   *Risk* by Tim Skeen. Selected by Gary Young.

Vol. 18   *What Euclid's Third Axiom Neglects to Mention About Circles* by Carolyn Moore.
           Selected by Patricia Spears Jones.

Vol. 17   *Notes from the Journey Westward* by Joe Wilkins. Selected by Samuel Green.

Vol. 16   *Still Life* by Alexander Long. Selected by Aliki Barnstone.

Vol. 15   *Letters From the Emily Dickinson Room* by Kelli Russell Agodon.
           Selected by Carl Dennis.

Vol. 14   *In Advance of All Parting* by Ansie Baird. Selected by Roo Borson.

Vol. 13   *Ghost Alphabet* by Al Maginnes. Selected by Peter Johnson.

Vol. 12   *Paper Pavilion* by Jennifer Kwon Dobbs. Selected by Genie Zeiger.

Vol. 11   *The Trouble with a Short Horse in Montana* by Roy Bentley.
           Selected by John Brandi.

Vol. 10   *The Precarious Rhetoric of Angels* by George Looney. Selected by Nin Andrews.

Vol. 9   *The Burning Point* by Frances Richey. Selected by Stephen Corey.

Vol. 8   *Watching Cartoons Before Attending A Funeral* by John Surowiecki.
           Selected by C.D. Wright.

Vol. 7   *My Father Sings, To My Embarrassment* by Sandra Castillo.
           Selected by Cornelius Eady.

Vol. 6   *If Not For These Wrinkles of Darkness* by Stephen Frech.
           Selected by Pattiann Rogers.

Vol. 5   *Trouble in History* by David Keller. Selected by Pablo Medina.

Vol. 4   *Winged Insects* by Joel Long. Selected by Jane Hirshfield.

Vol. 3   *A Gathering of Mother Tongues* by Jacqueline Joan Johnson.
Selected by Maurice Kenny.

Vol. 2   *Bodily Course* by Deborah Gorlin. Selected by Mekeel McBride.

Vol. I   *Zoo & Cathedral* by Nancy Johnson. Selected by David St. John.